SHARYN CRAIG

Layer 'em Up #3

Volume 3: Pinwheels & Points

Table of Contents

Layer 'em Up #3

Copyright © 2010 Sharyn Craig. All Rights Reserved.
Published by Cozy Quilt Designs™.
Printed in the United States of America.

Author: Sharyn Squier Craig
Publisher: Daniela Stout
Project Editor: Amy Falco
Graphics Editor: Amy Falco
Production Coordinator: Andie Stevenson
Operations Coordinator: Diane Lee

First Printing

ISBN: 978-0-9795316-9-9

sharyncraig@cox.net

Acknowledgments

As you sit reading a quilt book and enjoying all the pictures, you don't stop to think about all that went on behind the scenes to make a book happen. Without a large support cast I'd never be able to create a book, and you would not have the opportunity to enjoy the inspiration in these pages. So, I'm going to take just a few minutes to thank some of the people that made it possible for me to share this exciting concept with you.

First and foremost there's George, my husband of over 40 years . . . thank you for your constant love, support, and patience.

Then there's Amy, my daughter of nearly that long . . . thank you for your ability to take my scribblings and make them look and sound so professional.

I can't forget Daniela, my local shop owner, book publisher, and friend . . . thank you for allowing me to take these ideas and share them with quilters all over the world.

I'd never be able to do this without my Oncall Quilters, namely Sandy Andersen, Laurine Leeke, Marnie Santos, Carolyn Smith, Pat Hook, and Margret Reap. Thank you for making quilts for the book, for testing directions, for offering constructive criticism and suggestions that help me to be able to know the simplest way to explain things.

There are three very special ladies, Liz Henselmeier, Robin Ruiz, and Judi Sample, who machine quilted the quilts for this book. Thank you, thank you, thank you! I cannot begin to tell you how much I appreciate your amazing talents. Your quilting makes the quilts absolutely come alive.

I'd definitely like to thank the students around the country that worked through the designs, made quilts, and also helped with the pattern testing. A huge thank you for making me a better teacher.

To Sharron Armel, for allowing me to borrow the quilt she made in two of my workshops (Backgammon and X) that I've included in the gallery of quilts in the Backgammon chapter, thank you for being so generous! And, Andie Stevenson, thank you for making that first pinwheel quilt using my very early, very sketchy directions. If she could do it with those instructions, this book should make it a piece of cake!

To Moda Fabrics for providing much of the fabrics seen in the quilts made for this book. It was so exciting every time a package arrived. The Layer Cakes™ were so inspiring. They provided a color focus that I might not otherwise have taken.

I also need to acknowledge Pellon® who generously supplied me with a Legacy™ Soy Blend batting. It was fun to get the opportunity to experiment with a new product.

And last, but definitely not least, a special thank you to Maureen Cuddington for testing the written directions and making grammatical corrections.

~ Sharyn

Introduction

Sharyn Craig

I've been a quilter for over 30 years. I taught quilting many of those years. As a result I'm always looking for something a bit different, unique, and fun that I can share with other quilters. I no longer travel to teach, but I do still have the desire to share my ideas with quilters, so writing books is a fabulous outlet for this need.

The Layer 'em Up series began in the spring of 2009 with blocks that were related to the X design. In the fall of 2009, #2 came out. It focused on framed square designs. In Volume #3, the blocks are a bit more diverse, but still as exciting, and still utilize the same system of layering, slicing, scrambling, and sewing. The blocks are still very fast, extremely fun, and totally forgiving. The books are independent of one another, meaning each one stands on its own. You don't need to have worked through volumes #1 and #2 before starting on #3. Of course, I hope that if this is your introduction to the system you'll eventually want to look into the earlier volumes. But, rest assured, all the information you need to make the quilts found in this volume is here.

I love making these quilts. They are perfect for community service organizations, for prayer quilt ministries, for my grandchildren to nap with or build forts with — or even sleep under. I also like to use these patterns, and perhaps a more sophisticated group of fabrics, to make a more artsy quilt, perhaps for a wall. There is no limit to how you can use these designs.

Since the concept works so well scrappy, it is easy to start with the fabric I have at home, and then, if needed, add some new fabrics. Perhaps you'd rather start with a few new fabrics then round out the quilt from your stash . . . no problem!

The quilts in Volumes #1 and #2 all started with squares. Two of the patterns in #3 also start with squares. Backgammon and its variation, Fences, will start with rectangles. You can use Layer Cakes™, fat quarters, even yardage, to cut the necessary starting pieces.

You will soon notice that there is no yardage chart provided for any of the quilts. That's because I don't think in terms of yardage when making these quilts. What you need to know is that for every block you want to make you must have one starting square (or rectangle). If you want to make 40 blocks, you'll need 40 squares (or rectangles). What could be easier than that? If you decide to make the quilt larger than originally planned, all you need to do is cut more squares (or rectangles, see individual patterns). You can refer to the charts on pages 28 - 31 for guidance when determining how many blocks you need to make for whatever size quilt you want.

So, no more stalling, it's time to get in gear! Read on and prepare to be inspired.

NOTE

For every block you want to make you need one starting square or rectangle.

Basic Supplies

- **Sewing Machine** — Be sure to clean and oil your machine and replace the needle before beginning any new project.

- **Rotary Cutter** — You'll be cutting through lots of layers with these projects, so make sure your rotary cutter has a new, sharp blade. With each new project, a new blade is in order.

TLC for your rotary cutter:
Periodically you should take it apart and clean out all the lint that collects between the blade and the plastic shield. Once you clean out the lint, it is advised that you replace the oil that was there when you bought the cutter. The oil that you need is nothing more than sewing machine oil. One drop of oil before you put the blade back on the cutter will prolong the life of your blade dramatically.

Another thing that will make your cutter perform better is NOT to over tighten the screw when putting it back together. Here's a simple test you can perform: open your cutter and hold it lightly between your thumb and index finger. See if the blade turns freely and easily with no pressure or pushing. If you have to push the cutter to turn the blade, and there's no fabric involved, then imagine how hard you'll have to push when you have four or six or eight layers of fabric! If you have to use force to turn the blade, loosen the screw.

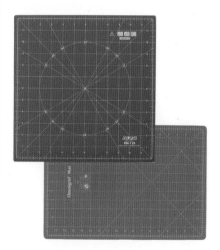

- **Mat** — When making these quilts, I really like the rotating mat by Olfa®. They come in different sizes, but the 12" square will work for all the blocks we make in this book. If you don't have an Olfa® rotating mat, then a small scale mat such as 12" x 18" will work.

- **Acrylic Rulers** — **Square Rulers and Strip Cutting Rulers**
Square Rulers: You'll definitely want to have a 10" square – such as the one by Cozy Quilt Designs™. You may also find it helpful to have other square rulers on hand, depending on the size block you choose to make, but you can square and true up your blocks to smaller sizes using the 10".

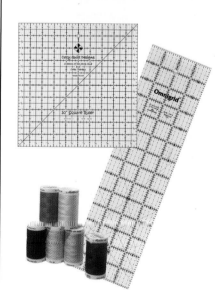

Strip Rulers: I suggest the 6" x 12", 2" x 18", or 4" x 14".

- **Thread** – I recommend high quality, 50 weight, 100% cotton thread.

Selecting Fabrics

These quilts can be whatever you want them to be: a whimsical quilt for a child, a sophisticated piece of art, a bed sized quilt for a grandchild bound for college (maybe in the school colors), or a couch quilt to match your family room. There are no boundaries. Let your imagination have wings and have fun with the process.

If you tend to become overwhelmed when picking fabrics for a project, you might find it easier if you start by selecting just one multi-color fabric. If you like this piece of fabric, then use the colors from it to select other fabrics, and colors, to go with it.

Look for a variety of print sizes and scales. You don't want all the same scale. Nor do you want all the same type of print. If you have some tonals (tone on tone, but all the same color), then you might want some plaids, some florals, some geometrics, in combination with the tonals. Variety of scale and type is what will add to the depth and richness of the finished quilt.

"STARTER" FABRICS

If you're drawn to a multi-colored piece of fabric, use that as inspiration when selecting your quilt colors. It doesn't have to end up in the quilt — or maybe you'll use it as the backing — but it's a great starting point.

Sometimes I start a new quilt by picking three or four colors that I like together, like red, green, and yellow. I'll pull a bunch of fabrics in each of those colors and fan them out on the table. As I do this I'm often inspired to add another color to the mix because of a particular fabric that introduces a new color. An example of this might be a black, red, green, and yellow floral, now I can add more black prints to the original grouping.

Because I've been quilting over 30 years, and collecting fabric the entire time, I could probably get away with never having to buy another piece of fabric as long as I live. Oh maybe for borders or backings, but not for blocks. But we all know that's not going to happen... me not buy any more fabric? It's not happening. I do still buy fabric. I find that new fabrics often make my stash more exciting. I love the pre-cut 10" squares. They are handy, convenient, and inspiring. I seldom use only the fabrics in one of these pre-packaged groupings, but it is a great way to begin.

NOTE

One of the great things about this technique is that you need one starting square for every one finished block you want to make. Look at pages 28-31 to determine how many blocks (and how many starting squares) you need for the size quilt you want to make.

All the quilts in this book have three things in common. They are fast, fun, and very forgiving. When you make blocks quickly, it is much less traumatic when one or two don't live up to your expectations. The bottom line here is that I want you to have fun making these quilts. So don't sweat the fabric selection. Relax and enjoy the process. If nothing else, you'll have a great community service quilt that can be given with pride, while you've enjoyed learning a new system for making blocks.

Fabric: To Pre-Wash or Not To Pre-Wash

Honestly, there is no right or wrong answer here. I have been making quilts for more than 30 years, and I have ALWAYS washed my fabric the minute it gets into the house; before it ever enters my sewing room. Having said that, there really is no good way to wash the 10" pre-cut square packages and the strip bundles, etc., that are on the market today, so I don't. To answer your next question, yes, I do mix my stash (washed fabric) with the unwashed 10" squares I buy.

I hear what you're thinking now, "But what's going to happen to my quilt when I wash it?" I am not going to be responsible for your quilts, but my personal experience has been that as long as there is plenty of quilting to hold the layers together, nothing adverse is going to happen. If you're worried about color bleeding, and who isn't, then you might put a Shout® Color Catcher® (available at many quilt shops and in your grocery store laundry aisle) in the washing machine when you wash the quilt. If there's any color loss, it will transfer to these Color Catcher® sheets, and not to other areas of your quilt.

Yardage

There are no charts in this book telling you how much yardage you need to make any of these quilts. Instead, you'll find charts on pages 28 through 31 to determine the size quilt you want to make with the size blocks you've chosen. You'll then know exactly how many blocks you will need to make. If you want 40 blocks, you will need 40 starting pieces of fabric (squares or rectangles depending on the pattern you're making). One starting piece of fabric is enough for one block.

I like working scrappy with 40 different fabrics to make up the 40 blocks I want. If you want a control fabric, as many of the quilts in this book have, then figure out how many total squares will be needed of that fabric (often it's half of the total). If you want 40 fabrics for the whole quilt, and 20 of them are to be the same light fabric, then figure out how many squares can be cut from one width of fabric. If you're starting with 10" squares, you should be able to get four squares per width of fabric. To get 20 squares you would need to cut five strips at 10" each. The total yardage needed would be 50" (1 ½ yards).

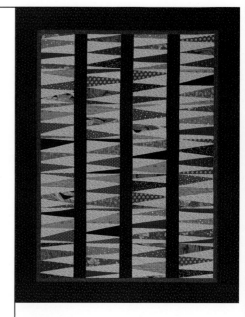

Bar None

See the Backgammon block, pages 20 - 25 for more information.

Basic Instructions For The System

Each of the quilt patterns in this book is based on a system of layering, slicing, scrambling, sewing, ironing, and squaring up. The descriptions that follow will help clarify each of these terms.

LAYER

First, you will position the suggested number of fabrics, one on top of another, slightly staggered. We're auditioning to make sure we like the fabrics in this order. You want to make sure you like the way each fabric looks next to the one it touches. Also, make sure you like the way the top and bottom fabric look together as they'll end up together in a block.

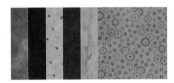

Next, position the fabrics so the edges line up as closely as you can.

(Six layers in this stack.)

SLICE

Slice through the layers as described in the individual pattern. A sharp rotary cutter blade will make this part of the process easier. If the pattern necessitates your turning the fabric to complete the slicing, you'll find that this is where the Olfa® rotating mat is a major help. You do not want to turn just the fabric. Turning the mat with the fabric in position allows you to cut easily and not have the fabrics shift.

HINT

Make sure your fabrics do not separate during the slicing process. They need to stay aligned.

SCRAMBLE

Once you slice the fabrics, you need to mix them up before sewing them together. You'll want to do this in a very organized manner. You'll see a Scrambling Diagram in each chapter. These diagrams have numbers on the pieces. Take the specified number of pieces from the top of each pile and move it/them to the bottom, as represented by the number on that piece in the diagram.

Example: If there is a zero (0), you leave it alone. If there is a one (1), take one piece from the top and move it to the bottom. A two (2) means move two pieces to the bottom, and so on.

SEW

Follow the numbered illustrations provided in the individual sections to sew the blocks together.

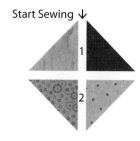

Start Sewing ↓

To keep your pieces in the correct order you need to follow these few simple steps:

1. Remove the block units from the sewing machine beginning with the last block unit sewn. Clip the units apart between the individual blocks, but not between the internal pieces of any one block, where applicable. (Example, the Hourglass block . . . the thread hinges at the center of the block keeps the individual pieces of any one block hooked together.)

2. Layer the block units one on top of another, starting with the last unit sewn, and ending with the first unit you sewed in the top position.

3. Finger press the seam allowance as suggested in each section. Press the pieces from the first block, then sew seam #2 by adding the piece on the right on top of the piece on the left. Finger press the pieces from the second block, then add the piece for seam #2 for the second block. Continue chaining the remainder of the blocks in this same manner.

IRON

Once the blocks are finished and sewn together, you can iron them firmly. Whether you use steam or not is up to you. Personally, I always use steam for a nice flat block. You always want to iron BEFORE you square-up the blocks. Iron from the wrong side first so you can control what is happening with the seam allowances. Then turn the block over, right side up, and do the final ironing.

SQUARE UP

The easiest way to square up your blocks is by using a square ruler the size of your finished blocks. Position the ruler on your block as desired, and trim all the way around. If you don't have the specific size ruler, then use the numbers on a square ruler that is larger than required.

HINT

Always begin at the left edge of the block and sew by positioning the piece on the right on top of the piece on the left, right sides together.

Finishing Instructions

I use a flannel wall to arrange my blocks, as blocks adhere to the flannel without having to use pins. I use solid white or off-white cotton flannel, available at many quilt shops as large as 108" wide, and simply thumbtack it to the wall at the ceiling and floor edges.

If you don't have an available wall to use, there are other options:

- Wrap your flannel around a purchased (or homemade) wooden stretcher frame and staple it to the back sides. Check your art supply stores for a blank framed canvas. I've been using a 3' x 4' one of these for years to take to workshops.

- If you can't find the 108" wide flannel, you might try a flat flannel sheet, or seam 45" wide flannel together to the size you need.

- Another possibility for your flannel wall is a sturdy cotton batting. These batts come in a variety of sizes so you can tailor them to fit your space.

LAY OUT YOUR BLOCKS AS DESIRED

Arrange your blocks to create the pattern of your choosing. Don't be afraid to play with your blocks. The quilts in each chapter are meant as inspiration. Feel free to change them around and see if you can come up with a totally different and unique design. Depending on your fabric choices and the arrangement, it is possible that no one would ever recognize your quilt as having been inspired by one found in this book.

Step back from the design and squint. Squinting allows your eye to see problems that might not be as visible otherwise. Some people like to look at their quilts through the camera for the same reason. Squinting, or looking through the camera at your quilt, will shrink the design and make some things pop, like strong fabrics too close together.

SEW THE TOP TOGETHER

Begin by sewing your blocks together into rows. I recommend alternating the seam allowances: row one goes all to the right, seams in row two all go left, three right, etc. Alternating the seam allowances this way allows them to butt up against one another and create a better fit.

Next, sew all the rows together.

IRON

Finally, iron your top carefully and thoroughly, being careful not to stretch or distort the edges. Check the top for flatness. Remove any stray threads that may be popping out of the seams.

BORDER

For these quilts, I suggest the following borders:

For 3" finished blocks:
- 1" cut size for the first border (Accent Border).
- 2 ½" cut size for the second border (Framing Border).

For 6", 7", 8", 10", and 12" finished blocks:
- 1 ½" cut size for the first border (Accent Border).
- 5 ½" cut size for the second border (Framing Border).

When attaching the borders, carefully pin at least every 5" to prevent the border strips from ruffling along the edges. I like to iron the border strip in place on the quilt, pin it, and then sew it. Ironing first helps prevent the ruffling as well.

Iron each of the border seams towards the border strip, away from the body of the quilt.

It doesn't matter whether you add the side strips first, or the top and bottom borders first, just be consistent.

Hourglass — Quilts to Inspire...

Reds and Greens Plus Cream

A scrappy packet of plaid fabrics jump-started this quilt. I layered them red, cream, green, cream . . . with the occasional red, cream, red, cream — and surprise black! Overall the quilt feels red and green, but that doesn't mean that I could or did, use only those colors. I layered only 4 fabrics at a time, which resulted in four identical Hourglass blocks. That was necessary to create the secondary pinwheel design you see in this quilt. I chose the strong color for the central pinwheel, and allowed secondary pinwheels to pop up throughout the quilt.

Super Scrappy *(set straight)*

I made all the blocks for this quilt and the on point sample below at the same time. I wasn't worrying about how many blocks I needed, I was just making lots of blocks. Then I started playing on the wall. I actually had extra blocks after making these two Super Scrappy quilts, but they'll find their way into other quilts someday I'm sure. To make these blocks I layered 8 fabrics at a time. I wanted the greatest diversity in the finished blocks as I could achieve. If you can't cut through 8 layers at one time, you'd still want at least 6 fabrics in any one grouping to result in no two blocks being the same.

Super Scrappy *(set on point)*

When you put the blocks on point, it creates a different feel. Now your eye tends to see half-square triangles, rather than the quarter-square version. You can make a larger quilt with fewer blocks when they are set on point. You will need the side and corner setting triangles to complete the design. You'll find the information needed for these triangles in the chart on page 31.

Hourglass — More Quilts to Inspire...

Super Scrappy in Rows
by Margret Reap

Who says you have to set all your blocks tangent? What if you put sashing between the blocks? What if you used the blocks as an alternating block between other focus blocks? Or, what if, like Margret, you positioned your blocks tangent in vertical columns, but then separated those columns with a sashing strip? It's such fun to see the variety of quilts you can create using the same, delightful little blocks!

Bunnies, Don't You Eat my Flowers!

You may have to look hard, but you'll find the Hourglass blocks in this quilt. I used a lot of similar green fabrics to create the background for my flowers and bunnies. The greens were layered just like the instructions in this chapter, then sliced and sewn into the Hourglass blocks. The pieced background is much more interesting than had I used a simple solid fabric. The quilt was made in response to a challenge that required the use of black, a neutral light, plus one other color, and we had to include at least one circle in the design. I love challenges that allow us creative freedom.

White Chili with a Dash of Cayenne Pepper

I love making white chili, especially when the weather is cooler. Every time I make it my husband reminds me to, "Not make it so spicy," which is of course not to use so much cayenne pepper. When I was working on this quilt, I couldn't help thinking about that. There was something about the colors that reminded me of the white chili. Two color quilts can be challenging to make, especially if you have the same number of each color in the quilt, and they are high value contrast. By using far more of the beige and tan fabrics with just a dash of the red I created a quilt that meets the criteria of a successful two color quilt. I stacked 8 layers to make this quilt . . . 7 tans and 1 red square per group.

HOURGLASS BLOCK

STARTING SQUARE	MEASUREMENT FOR SLICING	SQUARING UP SIZE	FINISHED BLOCK SIZE
10"	Corner to Corner	8 ½"	8"
9"	Corner to Corner	7 ½"	7"
8"	Corner to Corner	6 ½"	6"
5"	Corner to Corner	3 ½"	3"

NOTE: There is a difference of 2" from the starting squares to the finished block size. If you want a finished block size different than I've provided, all you have to do is add 2" to your desired finished block size to find the new starting square.

Use the chart at the top of this page to select the finished block size you want to make. Then, use the charts on pages 28 - 31 to select the size quilt you want to make and see how many total blocks you need to make for the size quilt you selected. If you want to make a quilt with 24 blocks, you'll begin with 24 squares of fabric, 48 blocks is 48 squares, etc.

LAYER YOUR SQUARES

Super Scrappy: Select six or eight starting squares of fabric. The fabrics can be high, medium, or low contrast. You can create the contrast through color only, or a combination of color and value. Make sure you can see some difference between the various layers.

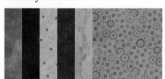

Controlled: Select four starting squares of fabric. Each grouping of four fabrics will be layered the same. The red and green double pinwheel variation (pictured on page 11) is an example of this controlled design. Each group of four fabrics was red, cream, green, cream, or in some cases, red, cream, red, cream. (I used more reds than greens in the total quilt.) In this quilt, each square was a different fabric, but you could have chosen to use the same cream fabric throughout.

Stack all the squares together, RIGHT SIDES UP, aligning the outer edges carefully.

The Hourglass block has been popular forever. The simple quarter-square triangle unit can be used, as seen in many of these quilts, as an all-over pattern set block to block. Or you can sash the blocks, or even use them as an alternating setting block with another more significant focus block. It might be fun to use these blocks as a border on another set of blocks. I love the way Margret used the Hourglass blocks as part of a bars set (pictured on page 12). It's hard to believe the quilts are all from the same set of squares, isn't it?

HINT

You may find it easier to oversize the original squares, stack, and then square to the starting size in the above chart. This makes it easier to cut perfectly corner to corner. When you can cut accurately corner to corner, you'll get more perfect finished blocks.

13

SLICE

Slice through the stack of squares, corner to corner, both ways, as illustrated.

SCRAMBLE

Using the following illustration, take the appropriate number of pieces from the top of the corresponding pile and move to the bottom. If you're doing the controlled version, you'll be making four identical blocks. If you're doing the Super Scrappy interpretation, there will be no two blocks alike, but in both cases the scrambling is the same.

SEW

Sew with a ¼" seam allowance when making all the blocks in the book. Follow the numbers on the illustration to sew your pieces together. Take the first two pieces that flank the #1 and position the triangle on the right on top of the triangle on its left. Sew from the point towards the center of the block, as indicated.

Start Sewing ↓

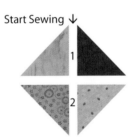

Continue with seam #2 by positioning the right triangle on top of the left triangle and sewing from the center towards the outer edge, as illustrated.

Continue with seam #1 on block number two, then number three, etc. You'll connect all the blocks in the stack this way.

NOTE

Remember, a zero (0) means leave that pile alone. A one (1) means you'll take one piece from the top and move it to the bottom. A two (2) means move two pieces to the bottom, and so on. The scrambling is the same, no matter how many squares you have stacked.

HINT

Always begin at the left edge of the block, and sew by positioning the piece on the right on top of the piece on the left, right sides together.

Clip apart between blocks, but NOT at the center of any one block.

← No Clip

✂Clip

← No Clip

Finger press the seam allowance (S.A.) as illustrated. Fold the block unit in half, using the thread hinge to keep the pieces lined up.

← S.A.

S.A. →

↓ Seam #3

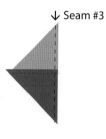

Sew the #3 seam. Repeat for the remainder of the blocks.

IRON

Once you've sewn the blocks you can go to the ironing board and iron them. Iron from the wrong side first so you can control what is happening with the seam allowances. Then turn the block to the right side and iron.

SQUARE UP

Refer to the chart on page 13 for the size to square up your blocks, based on the size starting square you began with. If you can't make your blocks the recommended size, don't worry, but do make sure all your blocks are the same size, whatever that is. With a seam in each of the four corners, it is an easy block for squaring.

Repeat all steps until you have made all the blocks for your quilt.

See page 10 for Finishing Instructions to complete your quilt top.

HINT

Clip the thread hinge — just snip that tiny thread that held the triangles together. This will allow you to alternate the seams in the middle, sometimes called "flowering." If you do this the same way in every single block, then when you sew the blocks together into the top (tangent, or block to block) every seam allowance will alternate and butt together perfectly throughout the entire quilt.

↑Clip thread hinge

S.A.

Pinwheel Variation — Quilts to Inspire...

Bright and Bold
by Sandy Andersen

The interaction between Sandy's bold blacks, the bright, fun colors, and the striking white dot fabric in this quilt create great energy. There are a total of 48 block units in this quilt, arranged into foursomes so the eye sees the 12 colorful pinwheels centered in each "block." Sandy chose to use only one white fabric, 12 different blacks, and 12 different bright fabrics. Her layering sequence was black, white, color, white. She needed a total of 48 squares, 24 white squares, 12 blacks, and 12 different colors.

Pastel Super Scrappy

This 48 block unit quilt is very scrappy, but reads controlled because of how I selected my fabrics. Peach and cream were selected as control colors, but then 12 other colors were picked for the central pinwheels in each 4-block unit. I layered my squares: peach, cream, color, cream. I chose 12 different peach fabrics, 24 different cream fabrics, and 12 different colors. You could create a very similar quilt using only one peach and one cream fabric — see what you have in your stash!

Patriotic Influence

This 48 block unit quilt is an example of using only 3 fabrics: one red, one blue, and one tan fabric. So when layering my four fabrics they were always the same order: red, tan, blue, tan. I arranged the block units to focus the red pinwheels in the center, but the blue and tan pinwheels are equally as strong. The design definitely tessellates across the surface of the quilt.

Autumn Leaves

Here is an example of one cream fabric, one floral fabric, and 12 different fall leaf colors. I chose my fall colors from my floral focus fabric — the catalyst for the entire quilt. Layering for the 48 block units was floral, cream, color, cream. I needed 24 cream squares, 12 floral, and 12 different fall colors. The color pieces are centered in each four block unit.

PINWHEEL VARIATION BLOCK

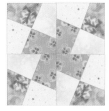

STARTING SQUARE	MEASUREMENT FOR SLICING	SQUARE UP SIZE	FINISHED UNIT SIZE	FINISHED 4 BLOCK SIZE
8"	2"	6 ½"	6"	12"
7"	2"	5 ½"	5"	10"
6"	2"	4 ½"	4"	8"
5"	1 ½"	3 ½"	3"	6"

Use the chart at the top of this page to select the finished block size you want to make. Then, use the charts on pages 28-31 to select the size quilt you want to make and see how many blocks you need to make for the size quilt you selected. Remember, if you want a quilt with 24 blocks, you'll begin with 24 squares of fabric, 48 blocks is 48 squares, etc.

One block unit doesn't stand on its own. The design in this pattern is dependent on four of these units going together, then this four block unit sitting next to another four block unit, etc. I personally feel the design is more successful when set straight, but I've no objection if you want to experiment with positioning the blocks on point, separating with sashing, or using in combination with other blocks.

LAYER YOUR SQUARES

For this pattern you will only layer 4 squares. You might want to study the quilts on the Inspiration page for color ideas and layering sequence. If you like the concept of using only three fabrics but you don't like the patriotic coloration, then substitute your color choices for the way I layered to create your own version.

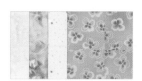

Make sure your squares are perfectly aligned. *(4 fabrics in this stack)*

NOTE

These starting squares really do need to be the same size, and stacked perfectly. To achieve that you may want to cut oversize squares first, stack, then cut to the starting size found on the above chart, prior to the slicing.

SLICE

Position your stack of squares on the cutting mat so the edges of the square line up with the lines on the mat.*

You'll be using the lines of your mat for the Measurement for Slicing (MFS). Position your ruler as illustrated, 2" to the left of the upper right corner, and 2" to the right of the bottom left corner, and slice.

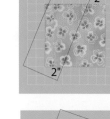

*If you're using the 5" starting squares, which have a 1 ½" MFS, position the squares so they don't line up with the lines, but instead visualize the half way mark. This allows you to still use the lines of the mat as your slicing guide.

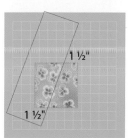

Rotate your mat one-quarter turn. Position the ruler the same way as illustrated, and slice.

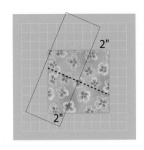

SCRAMBLE

Follow the numbered illustration to scramble the order of the pieces. Remember, a zero (0) means leave the stack alone, a one (1) means move one piece to the bottom of that stack, etc.

SEW

Using a ¼" seam allowance, and starting with seam #1, position the piece on the right on top of the piece to its left and sew from the outer edge towards the middle. Continue with seam #2 by positioning the piece on the right on top of the piece to its left. Repeat with block unit two, etc.

Take the units out of the machine and clip apart between the block units, but not at the internal hinge. Clip starting with the last block unit sewn, stack as you clip. You'll end up with block number one on top.

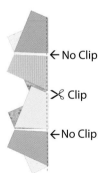

Finger press seam allowances (S.A.) as illustrated:

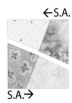

Fold and sew the remaining seam of each block.

Clip the blocks apart. Clip the hinge. Flower the seam allowance in the middle. (See HINT on page 15.)

IRON

Once you've sewn the blocks you can go to the ironing board and iron them. Iron from the wrong side first so you can control what is happening with the seam allowances. Then turn the block to the right side and iron.

SQUARE UP

Square up the individual block units according to the size indicated in the chart on page 17.

Arrange the four-block units as desired with the chosen color at the center of the blocks. Sew the four block units together the same way you sewed the four pieces to create one large block. Be careful with your seam allowances! By following these same steps, every single seam in your quilt top will alternate and butt up. There will be no stacked seams.

Repeat all steps until you have made all the blocks for your quilt.

See page 10 for Finishing Instructions to complete your quilt top.

Tessellating Pinwheels for Sophia
Andie Stevenson

Andie shares, "I made this quilt for my friend's beautiful, newborn twin granddaughter Sophia. Well, obviously there will be two quilts, but since Sophia was born before Adeline, this is her quilt. When I heard the twins would be girls, I got excited about pretty pinks and lavenders. I was quickly informed, no fru fru colors. The room would be in earthy jungle tones (browns, tans and olivey greens). I just knew I had to add some cheerful colors, so I chose orange and turquoise. I started with my stash and collected fabric from various shops, not knowing what pattern I was going make. I used 8 different prints and 6 different creams/tans. I just knew it would be scrappy, but organized scrappy. When Sharyn shared this block with me, I knew it would be perfect. I just layered colors together that I thought would work well with each other not really knowing how they would all come together. I stepped outside my own box, and this is the result. Now, I'm on to quilt #2 for Adeline."

Backgammon — Quilts to Inspire...

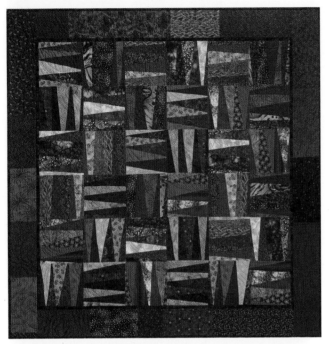

Red and Brown
by Margret Reep

Every time I look at this quilt I just want to lay down on the couch, cover up, and read a good book. Margret used regular cotton fabrics, but I think it would also be great in flannel plaids as well. The low contrast between the reds and browns contributes to the overall warmth of the quilt. There are a total of 36 blocks in this quilt, set 6 across and 6 down. For 36 blocks Margret needed a total of 18 different reds and 18 different browns. She set her blocks straight, alternating the direction of the pieces.

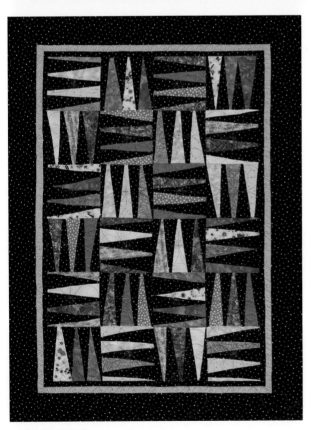

Royal Treatment
by Sharron Armel

The bold colors used here make this a royal and elegant quilt. Sharron took both my X and Backgammon workshops long before I knew I would be writing the Layer 'em Up books. She worked in the same colors both days and ended up putting the two sets of blocks together into one striking quilt: the X blocks used as a border around the Backgammon blocks. Her Xs were 6" finished blocks and the Backgammon blocks were finished 8". If you're interested in making Xs, check out the first volume of Layer 'em Up for directions. Or try using other combinations of blocks together!

Black and Bright

What kid wouldn't like this quilt? It's playful, whimsical, and just plain fun. There are a total of 24 blocks in this quilt, set 4 across and 6 down. To create these blocks I selected the black with bright dots fabric for a constant throughout, and cut 12 rectangles from this fabric. I then selected 12 different bright fabrics to accent the design. The blocks were set straight, alternating the direction of the spikes.

Hosanna

What if you set your blocks on point? That's exactly what I did with this set of 18 blocks. When I set them this way they reminded me of the Hosanna block, which is why I named the quilt Hosanna, reminiscent of the palm leaves and Palm Sunday celebrations. For this quilt I chose 1 light fabric and 9 assorted darks. Since each layered group has a total of 6 fabrics, this worked out perfectly. The layers were white, color, white, color, white, color. Sometimes, in order to make the number of blocks needed work out with the layering sequence, it is necessary to make a few extra blocks. Again, because we make the blocks so quickly, it isn't a big deal to have a few extras.

Spring Fever

Here's another on point example, but one that doesn't feel nearly as strong as Hosanna, due to the softer contrast in the fabrics. I used the same light print throughout, with a variety of blues and greens, accented occasionally with a yellow for punch. This quilt is also 18 blocks, on point, so 9 starting rectangles of the light control fabric, and 9 assorted blues, greens, and yellows. Remember to check the chart on page 31 for what size to cut the setting triangles depending on the size of your finished blocks.

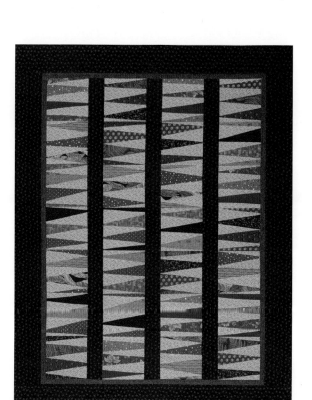

Bar None

What if you don't alternate the direction of the blocks? It's fun to think of the variations you can create if you let your imagination loose. This time I positioned the blocks in columns, but didn't worry which direction the spikes in any one block would point. There are a total of 4 columns with 7 blocks in each column; a total of 28 blocks in the quilt.

BACKGAMMON BLOCK

These quilts began for me with a challenge to create a variation of a Rail Fence block. Traditionally the Rail Fence block is shaded dark to light across the square. The sections are true rectangle in nature, and are often strip pieced. I asked myself, "What if I angled the ruler when cutting instead of cutting straight pieces?" It looked like a Backgammon board to me!

This block is definitely more random than most of the designs I've used in the Layer 'em Up Series. If you're more of a perfectionist or control person wanting every piece in your quilt to be more deliberate in size and shape, you probably won't be drawn to this pattern. You need to let go of expecting the pieces to be true points, or the same exact size. The way we make these blocks that is not going to happen.

STARTING RECTANGLE	MEASUREMENT FOR SLICING	SQUARING UP SIZE	FINISHED BLOCK SIZE
10" x 12"	Random	8 ½"	8"
9" x 11"	Random	7 ½"	7"
8" x 10"	Random	6 ½"	6"

Use the chart above to select the finished block size you want to make. Then, use the charts on pages 28-31 to select the size quilt you want to make and see how many blocks you need to make for the size quilt you selected. Remember, if you want a quilt with 24 blocks, you'll begin with 24 squares of fabric, 48 blocks is 48 squares, etc. In our example, half of those squares will be one color and half will be another color.

NOTE: Your blocks end up 2" smaller one direction and 4" smaller the other direction. This is because we only slice our blocks one direction. Even though we start with rectangles, we end up with squares. You can adjust for additional sizes by keeping these relationships in mind.

I recommend that you work with two main colors (or values). Study the quilts on the inspiration pages for ideas.

If you want to make a pink and blue quilt with 30 blocks total, you'd begin by selecting 15 different pink fabrics and 15 different blue fabrics. Remember, you can always choose to control rather than scrap the selection of fabrics. As you're picking your fabrics, you may think that throwing a few greens in with the blues would make it more interesting. That's what I did on the Bar None quilt when I added a few black prints into the mix with all those reds and greens.

LAYER YOUR FABRICS

Choose 3 rectangles from one color and 3 rectangles from your second color. Layer them up alternating the two colors.

Repeat with the rest of your rectangles, ALWAYS in groups of 6.

Stack all the squares together, RIGHT SIDES UP, aligning the outer edges carefully.

SLICE

You'll be making 6 random cuts, through all 6 layers, angling the direction of your ruler back and forth as illustrated. Make sure you're slicing the SHORT direction of the rectangles!

You want to make sure that you leave at least one-half inch at the narrow end between slices.

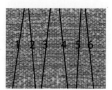

SCRAMBLE

Look at the numbers on the following diagram. These numbers tell you how many pieces of fabric to take from the top of each individual stack and move to the bottom of that same stack. Repeat with all the stacks, making sure to move the exact number it tells you to.

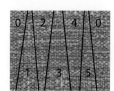 

By scrambling this way you'll end up with the finished block alternating colors, with the two end pieces being the same fabric. All other fabrics in between are different.

SEW

You will sew the blocks together from the left to the right. Always adding the piece on the RIGHT to the piece on the LEFT. Match the top and bottom edge when you begin and end sewing. Always sew with a ¼" seam allowance.

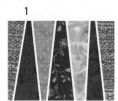 

HINT

If you're concerned about the "random" cutting, or that you might "run out of fabric" before you finish making your cuts, you might want to practice your cuts on a sheet of paper first. You don't have to actually cut the paper, you can use a pencil and just draw the lines in. This will give you a better feel for how much space to leave and how much to angle your ruler each time.

I personally like my blocks better when they aren't totally predictable, but if you need to have more control you can make a paper guide to position on top of each group of fabrics and cut on the lines.

NOTE: There are two options for sewing these blocks together.

- **By Block:** You can sew all the pieces in the top block together first, always adding the piece on the RIGHT to the piece on the LEFT, then the second block, the third block, etc. (This is the process we use here.)

- **Seaming Stacks:** You can seam all the pieces in the first and second stack (seam 1), then add on the third stack, the fourth, etc. (See page 9 in the Basic Instructions for more information on seaming the blocks together.)

It doesn't matter which process you choose, so long as you keep all the pieces that belong to any one block together. You want to end up with the two end pieces being the same fabric, but no other pieces in any one block being repeated. Keeping them in the order you established when you scrambled is important.

Finger press the seam allowance (S.A.) of the first two wedges towards the piece on right.

S.A.→

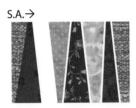

TIP

As you add each piece (RIGHT on top of LEFT) and sew, you'll be matching up one narrow end to one wide end (top/bottom). If you find otherwise, you've placed the pieces together incorrectly.

Position the next wedge on top and sew. Repeat with rest of units.

2

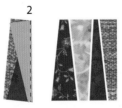

Continue sewing until you've sewn all the wedges together for the first block. Seam allowances are always guided to the right, or toward the piece you just added, which should be the piece on top.

S.A.→ → →

IRON

Iron the blocks from the wrong side first, keeping the seam allowances always going the same direction in any one block.

SQUARE UP

Reference the chart on page 22 to determine the square up size of the blocks according to the size of your starting rectangle. Feel free to manipulate your square up ruler on the block to create the best fit.

Repeat all steps until you have made all the blocks for your quilt.

LAY OUT YOUR BLOCKS AS DESIRED

Arrange your blocks to your liking on your flannel wall. Feel free to play and experiment. The quilts in this chapter are meant for inspiration, not limitation.

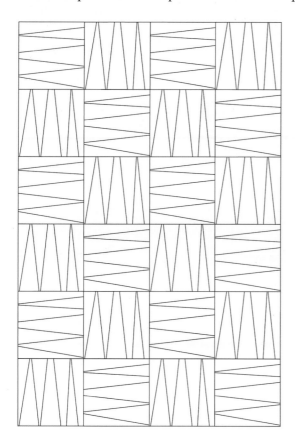

See page 10 for Finishing Instructions to complete your quilt top.

Fences — Quilts to Inspire...

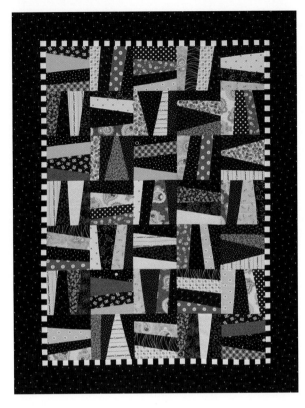

Mary Englebreit Inspired

A Layer Cake™ of Mary Englebreit fabrics by Moda inspired this quilt. I added a variety of black prints from my stash to give the quilt that extra punch. There are a total of 35 blocks in this quilt, set 5 across and 7 down. I layered 3 black prints with 3 of the bright prints, alternating the black and bright fabrics. You've probably already figured that I had one leftover block.

Citrus Sangria

The 24 blocks in this quilt are set 4 x 6. To create the blocks I chose 12 different cream prints and 12 assorted greens, yellows, and oranges. The quilt reminds me of slices of oranges, limes, and lemons floating in a refreshing glass of lemonade, or Sangria.

Trellis

This time I used two different Layer Cakes™ that provided the inspiration and fabrics for this quilt. The combination of different types of prints and intensity of colors — some brighter, some much more subtle — made for a very successful quilt. Like the Bar None quilt seen in the Backgammon chapter, I chose to position the blocks in columns. There are 4 columns with 7 blocks in each column, for a total of 28 blocks.

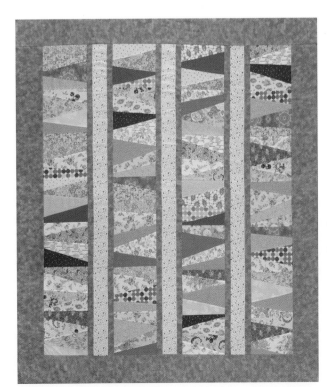

FENCES BLOCK

STARTING RECTANGLE	MEASUREMENT FOR SLICING	SQUARING UP SIZE	FINISHED BLOCK SIZE
9" x 10 ½"	Random	8 ½"	8"
8" x 9 ½"	Random	7 ½"	7"
7" x 8 ½"	Random	6 ½"	6"

This pattern is meant for inspiration. I'm giving you permission to play with my designs in different ways. This time I'm not going to give you all the step-by-step directions of the previous designs, but I will give you a starting rectangle chart and the basics needed. By now you should be able to take the ideas and run with them. The steps are very similar to the way Backgammon blocks were created. So, if you need to, you can always re-read those steps and go from there.

NOTE: Your block will change in size 1 inch in one direction and 2 inches the other. You can create blocks of other sizes keeping these proportions in mind.

LAYER YOUR FABRICS

4 – 6 layers, alternating colors or values.

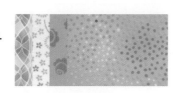

SLICE

Make 3 slices, randomly, across the SHORT direction of the rectangle.

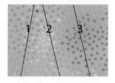

SCRAMBLE

Follow this illustration to scramble:

SEW

Like with the Backgammon block, you will sew the blocks together from the left to the right. Always adding the piece on the RIGHT to the piece on the LEFT. Match the top and bottom edge when you begin and end sewing. Always sew with a ¼" seam allowance, pressing the seams toward the piece just added.

IRON

Iron the blocks from the wrong side first, keeping the seam allowances always going the same direction in any one block.

SQUARE UP

Repeat all steps until you have made all the blocks for your quilt.

See page 10 for Finishing Instructions to complete the quilt top.

What if, instead of making six back and forth cuts as seen in Backgammon, we made only 3 slices? The result would be four chunkier wedges, but a very similar feel. Once I'd made several Backgammon quilts I started wondering what else I could do with the concept. Reducing the number of slices was one of the first things that occurred to me.

STRAIGHT SET

HOW TO USE THIS CHART:

The chart below shows you how many blocks you need to make the size quilt you want. If you already know the size you want to make, start by scanning the chart below to find that size, then follow that row over to the first two columns to see how many total blocks are needed and how they're set.

EXAMPLE: You want your finished quilt to be 60" x 68" with borders. You'll find that number in the 8" block column. You'll need 42 blocks, set 6 across x 7 down. This also shows you'll need 42 squares (or rectangles) of fabric to start your quilt.

NOTE: Finished top without borders shown in blue. Finished top with recommended borders (page 29) shown in red.

SET	TOTAL # OF BLOCKS*	FINISHED BLOCK SIZE					
		3"	6"	7"	8"	10"	12"
3 x 4	12	9" x 12"	18" x 24"	21" x 28"	24" x 32"	30" x 40"	36" x 48"
		14" x 17"	30" x 36"	33" x 40"	36" x 44"	42" x 52"	48" x 60"
4 x 5	20	12" x 15"	24" x 30"	28" x 35"	32" x 40"	40" x 50"	48" x 60"
		17" x 20"	36" x 42"	40" x 47"	44" x 52"	52" x 62"	60" x 72"
4 x 6	24	12" x 18"	24" x 36"	28" x 42"	32" x 48"	40" x 60"	48" x 72"
		17" x 23"	36" x 48"	40" x 54"	44" x 60"	52" x 72"	60" x 84"
5 x 7	35	15" x 21"	30" x 42"	35" x 49"	40" x 56"	50" x 70"	60" x 84"
		20" x 26"	42" x 54"	47" x 61"	52" x 68"	62" x 82"	72" x 96"
6 x 7	42	18" x 21"	36" x 42"	42" x 49"	48" x 56"	60" x 70"	72" x 84"
		23" x 26"	48" x 54"	54" x 61"	60" x 68"	72" x 82"	84" x 96"
6 x 8	48	18" x 24"	36" x 48"	42" x 56"	48" x 64"	60" x 80"	72" x 96"
		23" x 29"	48" x 60"	54" x 68"	60" x 76"	72" x 92"	84" x 108"
8 x 10	80	24" x 30"	48" x 60"	56" x 70"	64" x 80"	80" x 100"	96" x 120"
		29" x 35"	60" x 72"	68" x 82"	76" x 92"	92" x 112"	108" x 132"
9 x 12	108	27" x 36"	54" x 72"	63" x 84"	72" x 96"	90" x 120"	108" x 144"
		32" x 41"	66" x 84"	75" x 96"	84" x 108"	102" x 132"	120" x 156"
10 x 12	120	30" x 36"	60" x 72"	70" x 84"	80" x 96"	100" x 120"	120" x 144"
		35" x 41"	72" x 84"	82" x 96"	92" x 108"	112" x 132"	132" x 156"
12 x 14	168	36" x 42"	72" x 84"	84" x 98"	96" x 112"	120" x 140"	144" x 168"
		41" x 47"	84" x 96"	96" x 110"	108" x 124"	132" x 152"	156" x 180"

Total number of blocks represents both the number of squares to begin with, AND the number of finished blocks.

BORDERS

Straight Set 3 x 4

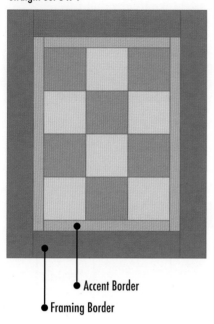

• Accent Border

• Framing Border

3" Blocks

• Cut 1" for the first border (Accent Border).
• Cut 2 ½" for the second border (Framing Border).

6", 7", 8", 10", and 12" Blocks

• Cut 1 ½" for the first border (Accent Border).
• Cut 5 ½" for the second border (Framing Border).

Type	Mattress Size	Basic Size (Including Borders)
Nap	n/a	48" x 60"
Crib	23" x 46"	36" x 48"
Twin	39" x 75"	60" x 96"
Full	54" x 75"	78" x 96"
Queen	60" x 80"	84" x 102"
King	72" x 84"	96" x 108"

DIAGONAL SET

HOW TO USE THIS CHART:

The chart below shows you how many blocks you need to make the size quilt you want. If you already know the size you want to make, start by scanning the chart below to find that size, then follow that row over to the first two columns to see how many total blocks are needed and how they're set.

EXAMPLE: You want your quilt to be approximately 60" x 80" with borders. You'll find something close to that in the 8" column. So follow that row over to the first two columns to determine how many blocks you need (39), and how to set them (4 across by 6 down), to get to that finished size. Since I have to always work in even numbers for the layering, my minimum number of starting fabrics (squares or rectangles) would be 40, even though the chart shows 39.

NOTE: Finished top without borders shown in blue. Finished top with recommended borders (page 31) shown in red.

SET	TOTAL # OF BLOCKS*	FINISHED BLOCK SIZE						# of Side Set Triangles Needed
		3"	6"	7"	8"	10"	12"	
2 x 3	8	8 ½" x 12 ¾"	17" x 25 ½"	19 ¾" x 29 ¾"	22 ½" x 34"	28 ¼" x 42 ½"	34" x 51"	6
		13 ½" x 17 ¾"	29" x 37 ½"	31 ¾" x 41 ¾"	34 ½" x 46"	40 ¼" x 54 ½"	46" x 63"	
3 x 4	18	12 ¾" x 17"	25 ½" x 34"	29 ¾" x 39 ½"	34" x 45 ¼"	42 ½" x 56 ½"	51" x 67 ⅞"	10
		17 ¾" x 22"	37 ½" x 46"	41 ¾" x 51 ½"	46" x 57 ½"	54 ½" x 68 ½"	63" x 79 ⅜"	
4 x 5	32	17" x 21 ¼"	34" x 42 ½"	39 ½" x 49 ½"	45 ¼" x 56 ½"	56 ½" x 70 ¾"	67 ⅞" x 84 ⅞"	14
		22" x 26 ¼"	46" x 54 ½"	51 ½" x 61 ½"	57 ¼" x 68 ½"	68 ½" x 82 ¾"	79 ⅞" x 96 ⅞"	
4 x 6	39	17" x 25 ½"	34" x 51"	39 ½" x 59 ¼"	45 ¼" x 68"	56 ½" x 84 ¾"	67 ⅞" x 102"	16
		22" x 30 ½"	46" x 63"	51 ½" x 71 ¼"	57 ½" x 80"	68 ½" x 96 ¾"	79 ⅞" x 114"	
5 x 7	59	21 ¼" x 29 ¾"	42 ½" x 59 ½"	49 ½" x 69 ¼"	56 ½" x 79 ¼"	70 ¾" x 99"	84 ⅞" x 118 ¾"	20
		26 ¼" x 34 ¾"	54 ½" x 71 ½"	61 ½" x 81 ¼"	68 ½" x 91"	82 ¾" x 111"	96 ⅞" x 130 ¾"	
6 x 8	83	25 ½" x 34"	51" x 68"	59 ¼" x 79"	68" x 90 ½"	84 ¾" x 113"	102" x 135 ¾"	24
		30 ½" x 39"	63" x 80"	71 ¼" x 91"	80" x 102 ½"	96 ¾" x 125"	114" x 147 ¾"	
8 x 10	143	34" x 42 ½"	68" x 84 ¾"	79" x 98"	90 ½" x 113"	113" x 141"	135 ¾" x 169 ¾"	32
		39" x 47 ½"	80" x 96 ¾"	91" x 110"	102 ½" x 125"	125" x 153"	147 ¾" x 181 ¾"	

Total number of blocks represents both the number of squares to begin with, AND the number of finished blocks.